One
Called
Wesak

A STORY OF FAITH

BY AL MINER AND LAMA SING

Library of Congress: 2018943355
ISBN: 9781941915165

1. Lama Sing 2. Psychic 3. Trance Channel 4. Death and Dying
I. Miner, Al   II. Title

Printed in the United States of America

For books and products, further information, or to write Al Miner
visit www.lamasing.org

THE FOLLOWING IS A SHORT STORY BY
LAMA SING, CHANNELED BY AL MINER.

IT WAS GIVEN MAY 12, 2003 IN ANTICIPATION
OF THAT YEAR'S WESAK FESTIVAL AND A LOOK
INTO THE JOY AND GLORY OF THAT ANNUAL
CELEBRATION

We are upon the gentle slopes of a large valley. Before us is a path which, as we look ahead, becomes more rugged. We are quite aware that it will be an arduous journey for those proceeding upwards upon it.

Soon we come upon a group of priests in scarlet robes who have a small throng of young adepts, young children, in their adorned in their own robes of bright saffron. They are all gaily making their way on a pilgrimage up this very massive mountain range before them.

As they proceed, the adepts, who are evidentially quite excited, are permitted to speak amongst themselves and, as well, to their revered teachers and guides.

One such teacher walks beside a young lad whom we shall call Wesak.

"Teacher? Do you believe that I shall be shown the path that is to be my destiny?"

Leaning upon his staff as he places one foot arduously before the other as they ascend, the teacher turns and looks down at Wesak, smiling. "It is not so important, my child, that I believe. Rather, it is do you believe?"

The lad, is bounding along upwards from foothold to foothold, as his response bubbles forth. "Oh, I believe, my teacher! I just wanted to hear you believe it."

With this, the teacher throws his head back with laughter, filling the narrow pathway, which has become now moreso like a ravine or gorge, carved out of the rock by some ancient stream or river no doubt.

"Then, know this my son, My belief and yours are as brothers."

They continue to make their way up the steep incline, the walls of the crevasse, the canyon, becoming steeper and more rugged. The hours pass, connecting one to the other, yet the spirits of these lads remain bright.

Suddenly, the priest at the lead raises his staff and hands upwards, and they all come to a stop. The young adepts crawl up to the front to where the priest has stopped and see that a massive hole has opened,

very deep and broad. They look to
the left and right, noting the steep
the walls of this pathway. There are
no footholds, no handholds, nothing
that might support their continuing
journey.

The disappointment of these
young ones is palpable, and there is
a moment's silence as all of them
along with the priests study their
leader at the forefront.

Finally, he turns to face them
and all are surprised to see that he
is smiling broadly. He raises his
hands and indicates that all seat

themselves wherever they can find a place to do so, for, remember, the area in which they have paused is very narrow and rugged. Then he, too, seats himself, ceremoniously moving his prayer covering from one shoulder to the other and placing his staff across his folded legs.

He leans forward with his hands together, and he offers a prayer. Bringing his hands up to his forehead, he salutes and offers a prayer unto God. "What a wondrous gift has been given unto us," he begins softly.

Wesak looks about, puzzled. The grand teacher notes this and smiles even moreso unto Wesak and nods, indicating for him to speak.

Wesak rises to his knees as bows as he places his hands in a respectful position over the center of his being. "Oh honored teacher, what is this gift you speak of? To my eyes and mind I see that the path cannot be traveled and that our journey upwards to the Temple cannot be completed." He seats himself and awaits the answer.

"The great gift here, my son, is of

many dimensions. It is," and he raises his hand to point to the new evening sky above them, "as the stars you see above, many of which have become more brilliant even as we are speaking. "You ask in your heart, 'How can it be so? We have labored all this day to reach this point only to be stopped, so it would seem, from reaching the Temple of Oneness with God.'

"These things do I offer to you, my children, and the others of you I invite you to find within: This is a gift of teaching of a magnitude that is such a blessing. For it is the exemplification of the journey through life, is it not, that as we might labor to reach a destination in life, indeed, we might find that something occurs before us of such a magnitude that we cannot transcend it.

"We can stop there in our journey, if our journey is also of spirit, in the intent of joy. And there we can dwell for the remainder of that lifetime, doing all that we know to do and the best we can do, and surely God would look upon this as a goodly work.

"And even though it seems

counter to many of the teachings we have shared with you, sweet children, another gift is to see in this same event that, to return upon one's pathway of ascent is not a great loss if one intends to find a more suitable path. So, you can journey back down the mountain, knowing that God will provide, perhaps not one but many other paths upon which the ascension to the Temple of Oneness with God can be reached. These paths might be known by some top the people here," gesturing to some of his brothers who are the priests on the periphery of the grouping, "or they might be known by others we do not yet know. If we seek out those we do not know, they may have the gift of ascension waiting to give it to us if we but ask them.

"So, we could remain here. We could build a new temple, perhaps making gentle this area before the great crevasse, constructing shrines and such according to our guidance and intent. Or we can descend and find other pathways to complete our joyful journey. And perhaps other gifts are within you, right this moment, waiting for you to ask for them."

The priest calls for all to join him in meditation. Small lamps are lit to soften the darkness that has descended, which seem to bring a warmth, a charm, a hopefulness, as the flames are reflected in the many soft colors upon the faces of this group.

At first, Wesak notes that the darkness within is not much different than the darkness without. Through his eyelids notes flickering, dancing light here or there, at least for a time. But then, as he has been taught, he moves beyond this to the embrace of God within.

He hears not a voice, nor does he see God, but this he sees ... He sees an old man seated upon this very pathway, greeting passersby as they journey here to reach the Temple of Oneness atop this mount. At first, he shakes himself. How can this be, for his mind tells him such a crevasse upon this pathway cannot be transited. No one could possibly pass this way. Yet when he stills these thoughts, he still sees the aged one sitting, smiling, greeting the journeyers as they pass him by giving unto him their alms and their blessings.

Again, Wesak shakes himself, this time to pay attention to the question and doubt from his mind, from his heart, from his spirit. He knows these to be the veils of illusion that strive to make their offering to him and that, in the understanding of these, he knows he will discover himself.

So, one by one he looks upon them, facing them.

Doubt: "The chasm is too great. This vision is not possible. Wesak, turn away."

In his spirit, Wesak answers, "Naught is too great for God, and those who are one with God are empowered to meet any such that is brought to them."

The of doubt veil then moves away from him.

Next, a swirling grayish dark mass of undulating energy, appears and, in it, a face.

Wesak looks upon the face. "I love you. You are my voice of reason and I honor you. But know this: Faith is the tool and the power that I apply."

The veil of reason bows to Wesak. "Thank you, Wesak, for your honor. I, Reason, love you as well."

Again and again, the challenges of limitation, the forces of habit, the thoughts of logic, and so on, come to offer their gift to Wesak, and each time He thanks them and gifts them with his love.

To an observer, it may be curious that they do not scorn Wesak, they do not continue to challenge him nor struggle to sustain dominion.

Rather, that honor which Wesak gives to them, they return to him.

Now cometh a light unto Wesak, as many veils have been parted. The light takes form and steps forward as a luminous being, an angelic messenger of God. The angel bends and speaks directly into Wesak's ear.

Wesak begins to smile. "Yes! Yes!" he answers. "I will do this. I can do this."

Finally, the gentle sounds of chimes call all back into the world of the journeyer called Life.

Wesak looks about and smiles broadly. All of the children are bright, for each has seen their journey.

The elder priest looks about and then rests his gaze upon Wesak, for he sees the light of God around him. "Ah, little Wesak ... You have been visited, I see?"

Wesak kneels, offering a salutation from his place of honor, which is just above the center of his being. "Yes, my Lord."

"Then, shall you journey down

the mount and seek another path, or shall you stay here," gesturing with his hands to the left and right, "and strive to do what can be done?"

All are silent, smiling expectantly at Wesak, for all present see the light about him.

"I shall do both, my Lord, and the greater," responds Wesak.

The elder teacher raises his hand. "Praise God. And praise you, Wesak, for I see your intent. Speak no more. Do as you know to do."

Most of the group, upon resting, begin the arduous journey back down the pathway to the gentler slopes below. Some move in various directions, traveling to seek out farmers or villagers who might know of another path. Others follow several priests who already know of such a path. It is one filled with danger and hardship, but it is a path, nonetheless.

But before any of these separate to being these journeys, they pause and turn to look up the path, for the elder priest is calling out. "Wesak, which is your choice of journey? How do you intend to find, from the voice of God's Oneness in the Temple atop this mount, the destiny awaiting you?"

Again, Wesak kneels and salutes the priest. "My Lord, you gifted me with the accomplishment of my intent for my ascension of the Mount of Oneness."

Some of the other adepts look at one another for, clearly, none have reached the summit. None have entered the Temple of Oneness atop this mount. What can it mean, that their brother speaks?

But the priest knows, and smiles, nodding at Wesak. "You have found your destiny, your service? Your work of joy and fulfillment?"

"I have. In the temple, here." Wesak taps his heart.

The priest turns to look over the group. "Are there others of you who would join Wesak, even though you know not the nature of his intent? Open yourselves now to feel what it is that he knows. Then, so as you are called to join him, to stand at his side, answer it. If your journey takes you elsewhere, answer and equally honor that."

Wesak moves down the slopes of the this mount and out into the plains. Several others who have heard the same call and choose to remain with him, along with some of the teachers, follow, smiling in prayerful countenance.

As he comes to farmer after farmer who are clearing their fields of rocks and stones and such, he asks of them these simple words, "Good sir? I see you have discovered these gifts from God. May I, and my honored brothers and revered teachers, take these as gifts back to God?"

Some of the farmers remove their hats and scratch their heads, and look down at the many different sized stones before them thinking, "He considers these stones to be gifts of God??" But looking back up and into the eyes filled with love and hopefulness, they question him not, and answer with surprising exuberance. "Tell us but where you would like these gifts of God to be placed, young priest, and we shall honor you and God by delivering them to that place."

Again and again, this transpires.

Finally, Wesak and his handful of brothers and the teachers with him are seated by the path which leads up the rocky crevasse to the great chasm upon the pathway of ascension beyond. But now, great piles of various sizes of stones lie positioned along the path — so many and more coming, as the farmers clear their fields, joyful to be rid of these gifts of God and joyful that they are appreciated by this young lad. They are energized by his exuberance and they receive his prayer and those of his colleagues for each stone they bring.

Wesak, now, sends two of his colleagues, young adepts, along with a priest, to rise the arduous path, telling them to position themselves at the crevasse above where the great chasm has opened upon the path of ascension.

Now, travelers to the mount, who know not of the great chasm upon this path, come upon Wesak and his remaining brothers. He greets them with, "Bless you, good traveler, on your journey. You seek oneness with God, is it true?"

They nod and smile.

Wesak continues. "The path ahead is difficult, and to some degree, unexpected, but blessings await you. I would ask of you a gift."

The travelers, in their anxiousness to reach oneness with God atop this mount, and seeing the holiness of this young priest and his companions, respong, "You have only but to ask of us and we shall do it."

Rising, Wesak walks along the massive piles of stones now collected along the sides here.

"Look you upon these. Some are of this size," gesturing to a pile of sizeable boulders, "and there are differing sizes, down to ..." and he points to a pile of pebbles. "Choose, you among these that which you would bear as gifts to God for your journey's end."

Again and again, travelers come and the same message is given and, with joyful expectancy, not knowing why a stone would be considered a gift unto God, they choose according to their guidance from the stones of varying sizes. Some choose such that are so large and so heavy they can barely ascend carrying them. Others choose a handful of pebbles here and there and continue on.

As they journey up the crevasse and reach the chasm, the priest and adepts greet them. Here, they have prepared the traditional ceremonies of blessing to travelers, and they are carefully making special prayer shawls, small strips of cloth with prayers written in the sacred writing of the temple priests to be given as gifts to the journeyers.

One after another reaches the

edge of the vastness of the chasm that has opened. And again and again, the traveler, such as this one, who has turned to the adepts and the priest. He states, a hint of frustration and disappointment in his voice, "The young priest below spoke not of this impossible hole, but only that gifts and blessings would await us."

The priest answers softly, "Have you brought gifts unto God?"

"Yes," this traveler comments, bringing forth two sizeable stones, one in each hand.

"Then throw them in here," gesturing to the great hole, "and as you do, know that thou art blessed. Then pause a time here with us, and we shall pray and meditate with you, that the answer to your quest is given you."

And so, each traveler, one after the other, does the same, closing their eyes a moment and then throwing their gift-stones into the great chasm. They, then, meditate and pray with the priest, and the priest lights incense and speaks prayers and rings his chimes, finally placing the prayer over the traveler's shoulder.

Each traveler's face is illuminated with the revelation of something they sought, each one caresses and looks upon the prayer so lovingly created and blessed by these young adepts and teachers, and returns from whence they came.

So it did come to pass that, in the many decades that transpired, this pathway, which was once so difficult to ascend, became worn by the feet of the travelers, many thousands of them who came and went bearing the stones as gifts to God, into one which could be ascended with relative ease.

Now, at the edge of the great chasm, sits an elderly priest — his hair as white as the purity of the cap of snow atop the Mount of Oneness, his eyes aglow with the accomplishment of a lifetime of service, his shoulders covered with prayerstrip upon prayerstrip. And to his right and left, bowls of this and that given by those who made their pilgrimage to the top of the holy Mount of Oneness.

Just beyond him, the great chasm, the huge hole, that was upon this path of ascension, is no more, for it is filled with the gifts given unto God by the decades of travelers who have tossed their gift-rocks into this hole, so many so that the hole is now as one with the path, once again. Those who now seek to ascend unto Oneness can do so with ease as they travel across the beautiful array of stones of all different sizes that have filled this great chasm and made the way passable.

It shall come to pass that God shall call upon His son, Wesak, to return from this journey. But not just now, for he reaps the harvest of his faith as he looks into the eyes filled with hopefulness and love of God of each who makes this pilgrimage to ascend the Mount of Oneness.

Looking upon the chasm filled with the beautiful gifts of God of the stones which have now made the way passable, they turn to Wesak and he gives unto them according to the guidance of God within.

But always he says unto them, "Look you, brother, sister ... This way was once impassable. But each small gift unto God, given by one who came before you, has made the way passable for you.

"Perhaps, as you journey on, you will think on this and give a blessing or two unto those who have gone before, in memorial of their service unto you and to God. And perhaps, as you do this, you will listen and hear them giving unto you their on memorial, their testimony unto your faith that you should labor to make this journey.

"For as you ultimately reach your destination of Oneness with God, they shall be there, awaiting you."

You can find much, dear brothers and sisters, in this small tale that might give you cause to look upon what has been shared here and to see this ceremony of faith and dedication as an inspiration for your own life.

Whether it is a pebble small enough to be carried in the palm of your hand or a stone seen as being so great that you are barely able to carry it, each is an equal gift: If you have the faith of one such as Wesak and throw it into that chasm which seems to limit your pathway, it shall come to pass when the obstacle, which has been seen as a great chasm separating you from God, is filled, and the way is opened. No matter how long the journey, how great the labors, or the length of time involved, if you meet these and *welcome these* with the faith of Wesak, this is likened unto him welcoming each veil that attempted to separate him from the truth of God and the accomplishment of his life's work.

As those who made their pilgrimage looked into the eyes of Wesak, they were inspired to see those inert objects called stones of all different dimensions, shapes, and sizes, truly as gifts. So they faithfully bore them unto that destination without knowing that these tributes of faith would ultimately build a pathway for their own ascension in future journeys, as well as to make the path open and passable for others who would follow them.

———

So the celebration called the *Wesak Festival,* which is the coming together of the Active and the Passive, the Feminine and the Masculine, and all of the other descriptions or titles which can be aligned to these polarizing forces, is summarized in the ceremony which takes place. It is where the Christ and the Buddha, the great saints, and all the faithful gather to bring into the Earth a ray of hope and to illuminate those rays of light and understanding. Not just one of these Blessed Ones is giving, but all. For many believe there is but one path and often feel they journey alone. This is a veil that needs to be spoken to, to be given name, to be honored, and to be told that it is loved, in order that the truth can be seen and the way can be opened.

To those who have seen each of the challenges that have been met not as painful or bad (betrayal, hardship, a sense of loss, grief, and all that sort), but as gifts of God, bringing forth these potential limitations and transforming them into the step-stones of ascension, these are at the forefront.

So it is with our love, and our encouragement to each of yo, that we have offered this remarkable memorial unto a young man of few years but of profound wisdom whom we have called Wesak. There is, you see, after all, one such within each of you who, in the moment of recognition of each veil of separation, can do just the same — meeting any challenge, any obstacle, do so with the faith and with the youthful expectation and hopefulness of one called Wesak.

We give thanks unto all of you, dear friends, for your faith, for your dedication, and for your love, that the light of the new dawning of expectation may ever warm you from within and shine forth to illuminate your path. Fare thee well, then, for the present, dear friends.

BOOKS BY AL MINER & LAMA SING

The Chosen: Backstory to the Essene Legacy
The Promise: Book I of The Essene Legacy
The Awakening: Book II of The Essene Legacy
The Path: Book III of The Essene Legacy

In Realms Beyond: Book I of The Peter Chronicles
In Realms Beyond: Study Guide
Awakening Hope: Book II of The Peter Chronicles
Return to Earth: Book III of The Peter Chronicle

Death, Dying, and Beyond: How to Prepare for The Journey
Vol I
The Sea of Faces: How to Prepare for The Journey Vol II

Jesus: Book I
Jesus: Book II

The Course in Mastery

When Comes the Call
The Children's Story

Seed Thoughts
Seed Thoughts to Consciousness

Stepstones: Compilation 1
Stepstones: Compilation 2

Wesak

For a comprehensive list of reading transcripts available,
visit the Lama Sing library at www.lamasing.net

About Al Miner

A chance hypnosis session in 1973 began Al's tenure as the channel for Lama Sing. Since then, nearly 10,000 readings have been given in a trance state answering technical and personal questions on such topics as science, health and disease, history, geophysical, spiritual, philosophical, metaphysical, past and future times, and much more. The validity of the information has been substantiated and documented by research institutions and individuals, and those receiving personal readings continue to refer others to Al's work based on the accuracy and integrity of the information in their readings. In 1984, St. Johns University awarded Al an honorary doctoral degree in parapsychology.

Al conducts a variety of field research projects, as well as occasional workshops and lectures. He is no longer accepting requests for personal readings, but, rather, is devoting his remaining time to works intended to be good for all. Much of his current research is dedicated to the concept that the best of all guidance is that which comes from within. Al lives with his wife on the Florida Gulf coast.